A Taste of Heligan
fish, meat, chicken and game recipes

PAUL DRYE

First published in 2004 by Truran, Croft Prince, Mount Hawke, Truro, Cornwall TR4 8EE
www.truranbooks.co.uk

Truran is an imprint of Truran Books Ltd

ISBN 1 85022 187 1 (p/b)
ISBN 1 85022 188 X (h/b)

Printed and bound in Cornwall by
R. Booth Ltd, Antron Hill, Mabe, Penryn, Cornwall TR10 9HH

Other books in this series:
A *Taste of Heligan – vegetarian and fruit recipes* Richard Quested and Paul Drye
A *Taste of Heligan – the best from the bakery* Tina Bishop and Paul Drye

Thanks once again to my wife Angela for all her typing, tasting and loving enthusiasm and to our dear friends Debbi Baldanza and Jimmy for their much valued IT support and their shared enthusiasm for Italian cuisine, wine and culture.

Thanks to the entire catering team at Heligan for their good humour and hard work. A special mention goes to Tina, Simon, both Carols, Mary, Katy, Kieron, Selim and Heather whose craft skills, reliability and dedication keep the catering engine running as smoothly as it does and who contribute to a product we can all be justly proud of. Thanks also to the Gardening Team – in particular: Beki, Jeremy, Katharine, Charles, Clive, Sylvia, Helen and Mike and the Home Farm Team – Malcolm, Brian and Craig for their knowledge and skills in those wonderful ingredients which inspired me so much in these recipes; a final word of thanks to Candy Smit for her continuing enthusiasm and support throughout this project and to Snappy Stephens for his photography.

The Willows Tearoom/Restaurant is open to garden and non-garden visitors throughout the year from 10am daily, closing half an hour before the gardens.

The gardens are open all year round from 10 am daily
The Lost Gardens of Heligan, Pentewan, St Austell, Cornwall PL26 6EN
Tel: 01726 845100   www.heligan.com

Introduction

Having been a chef here at Heligan for many years it gives me great pleasure to share some of my favourite recipes in this, the third A *Taste of Heligan* book. This time I have been inspired by our beautiful Heligan reared meat, the fine beef and lamb also produced by our neighbouring farmers, the freshest fish from Cornish waters and local wild and farmed game. Chefs here have the task of marrying these superb ingredients with the abundance of fresh fruit, vegetables and herbs harvested seasonally at Heligan by our dedicated team of gardeners – I've said this before and I'll say it again – this truly is Chef's Heaven!

These recipes are quite varied – some are influenced by the fresh produce available throughout the changing seasons, others have taken exotic spices to add warmth and excitement; there are dishes to comfort you on cold winter nights and others to enjoy with friends on balmy summer evenings.

All of these recipes have been tried and tested here at Heligan where they were greatly appreciated by our Feast Night diners. Some are classic dishes, others are my own original recipes developed and inspired during my time at Heligan. All methods are simple to follow and produce mouth-watering results. If you start with the freshest of ingredients you can't go wrong.

The first step to finding the best produce is to buy locally. Food that has travelled hundreds or even thousands of miles and been picked a week or more previously quickly loses its flavour and goodness. Therefore I firmly believe locally reared meat and seasonal vegetables, fruit and herbs are far superior. Cooking with such ingredients is a pleasure only surpassed by eating the results. Once you get passionate about your ingredients, eating becomes one of life's greatest pleasures.

Here at Heligan we practise what we preach. If we can't produce something ourselves we buy locally – if it can't be produced in Cornwall we buy through a Cornish company. It's a two-way thing: we support local businesses in the community and in return we cook with the best produce Cornwall has to offer. Truly a win-win situation.

In recent years with the development of the Home Farm here at Heligan, I have had the privilege of cooking with some of the finest quality meat I have ever come across: succulent, tender cuts of meat with just the right amount of fat, hung for a good length of time and butchered with care and skill.

I learnt to appreciate good meat from an early age working in a traditional butcher's shop whilst still at school. I started with sausage making and moved on to boning and jointing lamb and pork and eventually on to the finer, more expensive cuts of beef. Working with a pair of formidable old gents – master butchers who had been in the same profession for sixty years, I soon noticed our meat was darker through being well-hung, unlike the bright red supermarket joints. As a result our meat was tender, with a rich flavour and therefore needed less cooking. We sold meat to many local restaurants, in one of which I was later to become commis chef – the start of a long career which eventually led me to Heligan, where my passion for cooking good quality meat is stronger than ever.

In the years that passed in between, I became chef pâtissier and sous-chef and eventually held the position of head chef in a number of excellent restaurants before turning to catering management, working for a large corporate catering management company. This gave me a varied career in which I cooked for society weddings at Highclere Castle in Berkshire, and on another occasion found myself on a tasting panel with the enviable job of being paid to drink beer! But making good food with the best ingredients for appreciative customers is what I will always love to do.

After singing the praises of local produce please remember when using these recipes that 'local' means food that is local to you. Every county has its own specialities and regional produce – so get out there, discover them and love them!

In the recipes that follow I have included good quality stocks, an abundance of fresh herbs and used only fresh vegetables. But these recipes are just a guide, as I always say: 'rules are meant to be bent if not broken' where cooking is concerned. A few dried herbs and a tin of tomatoes in a sauce is nothing to be ashamed of. You can't beat a properly made stock but don't beat yourself up over a stock cube! Enjoying yourself is what cooking should be all about. So invite some friends, put on some music, and uncork the wine. In life one can never tire of these simple things.

I wish you the best of luck with your cooking.

Paul Drye

The Recipes

Starters

Soups

Fish

Beef

Lamb

Pork

Chicken

Game

Pork and Pickled Peppercorn Pâté

These days at Heligan the chefs often use meat raised on the estate. But I remember when the very first pigs arrived, all the catering staff were quite excited – not from a culinary point of view; but the idea of feeding them leftover cakes every afternoon was an opportunity too good to miss. For many months a steady stream of scones, carrot cake, shortbread, flapjack etc was paraded down to our pigs – needless to say it was quite a shock to us all when one day four pigs arrived at the kitchen all ready for my freezer! I must say those first pigs had a good layer of fat on them giving the best crackling I have ever tasted – well they were scone-fed! Unfortunately recent changes in legislation mean that it is now illegal to feed cakes to pigs!

For 8+

450g/1lb diced shoulder of pork
450g/1lb sliced pig's liver
55g/2oz butter
110g/4oz chopped onion
2 tablespoons olive oil
5 cloves of garlic
120mls/4fl oz red wine
570mls/1 pint of good chicken stock
2 leaves of gelatine (optional)
4 teaspoons of pickled peppercorns
a few sprigs each of parsley, thyme and rosemary
salt and pepper

This may seem like a lot of pâté but if you are going to the trouble, why not freeze some?

Heat the oil in a large saucepan, fry off the pork, onions and liver for 10 minutes. Add the garlic cloves whole and cook for a further 2 minutes. Add the red wine, chicken stock and bring to the boil giving a good stir. Wash the herbs and pluck from their stalks, add unchopped to the pan. Season with a little salt and pepper and cover with a close-fitting lid. Bring to the boil and simmer gently for 2 hours stirring every 20 minutes and adding a splash of water if the mixture begins to dry out too much. The aim is to get a mixture that is cooked but not too wet – this can be achieved by removing the lid during the last 45 minutes of cooking to reduce the liquid – you may also add a couple of leaves of gelatine at the end to help your pâté to set.

When you are satisfied that all of the meat is tender pass the mixture through a mincer or whizz in a food processor. After mincing add the pickled peppercorns, stir thoroughly and pour the mixture into a suitable earthenware dish and smooth over. Place in a refrigerator for 1 hour then melt the butter and brush over the top before refrigerating for a further 4 hours or overnight. (The butter will help prevent discolouring of the surface.) Serve with hot buttered toast and Cumberland Sauce.

Oak Smoked Chicken with Avocado

As starters go this is deliciously simple. The locally oak smoked chicken we use is just superb. If you can find a smokehouse near you then give them a visit, it's certainly worth it. We also use smoked salmon, cheddar, ham and gorgeous smoked pork, apple and cider sausages – all produced just a stone's throw from Heligan. In this recipe the smoky flavour of the chicken contrasts with the creaminess of the avocado. This is complemented beautifully with a smooth Sauce Tyrolienne.

For 4

2 oak smoked chicken breasts
2 avocados
4 sprigs of parsley
4 nasturtium flowers

For the Sauce Tyrolienne:
4 tablespoons of mayonnaise
30g/1oz onion
splash of olive oil
3 tomatoes
small sprigs of parsley, thyme, chervil and tarragon

Finely slice the onion, chop the herbs for the sauce and cook all in a hot pan with a splash of olive oil until the onion is soft. Add the skinned tomatoes, finely chopped, and cook until soft and quite dry, then remove from the stove and allow to cool. Whizz the cold tomato mixture in a food processor with the mayonnaise. This should give you a smooth pink sauce – Sauce Tyrolienne!

Thinly slice the chicken breasts, then stone, remove from the skin and thinly slice the avocados. Arrange the chicken and avocado slices, alternating in a fan shape onto four plates. Spoon some of the Sauce Tyrolienne by the side of each fan and garnish with a sprig of parsley and some nasturtium flowers. You need nothing to go with this – just enjoy the texture and contrast of tastes.

Beef and Smoked Garlic Cannelloni

Smoked garlic has got to be one of my favourite ingredients. Garlic on its own is good, wild garlic is excellent, but smoked garlic is just heaven. With its heady aroma and distinctive creamy, mild, sweet taste, it lends itself to so many dishes. If you have already used smoked garlic you will know how wonderful it is. If not, then a culinary revelation is waiting out there poised to seduce your senses. Just go out there and find some!

For 4

Sauce:
1 large onion
2 cloves of smoked garlic
1 jar of passata (smooth sieved tomatoes)
1 tablespoon olive oil
1 tablespoon tomato purée
10 basil leaves
8 sprigs of oregano
1 small bunch of parsley
salt and pepper

Filling:
12 cannelloni verde tubes
450g/1lb lean minced beef
6 cloves of smoked garlic
1 tablespoon of olive oil
1 beef stock cube
salt and pepper
a little of the above sauce
110g/4oz mozzarella

First make the sauce – heat the oil in a saucepan, finely dice the onion and fry gently without colour for 5 minutes. Add crushed garlic, and fry for a further 3 minutes. Pour in the passata, add the tomato purée,

stir, bring to the boil and simmer gently for 20 minutes. Wash and chop the fresh herbs, adding half to the sauce at the very end of cooking, with salt and pepper to taste. Remove from the heat and set aside.

Now for the filling – heat the olive oil in a large frying pan, add the lean mince and fry for 15 minutes, stirring throughout. Crush the smoked garlic cloves and add to the mince along with the stock cube and the remaining fresh herbs. Cook for a further 5 minutes, remove from the heat, and whizz in a food processor for 30 seconds.

Now, add a little of the sauce and whizz for a further 10 seconds. The consistency you are looking for must be soft enough to pipe but stiff enough to stay inside your cannelloni. Season to taste and allow to cool for 15 minutes before spooning into a piping bag with a large plain nozzle. Fill the cannelloni tubes and place in a square earthenware roasting dish, pour the sauce over, followed by slices of mozzarella spread evenly over the top.

Bake in a preheated oven 190°C/375°F/gas 5 for 25–30 minutes until pasta is tender and the top is golden brown and bubbling. Serve immediately with a crisp leafy salad and a light fruity red wine.

Chilli Crab Cakes

Made with the very best locally caught crab and our own chillies grown in the Citrus House located in the Flower Garden. These spicy little devils are kept in their place with a cool mint and cucumber raita; perfect, as here as a starter or you can always make them bigger and serve them as a main course with a squeeze of lime.

For 4

Crab Cakes:
225g/8oz cooked crabmeat (brown and white flesh)
110g/4oz mashed potato
110g/4oz cooked long grain rice
3 whole fresh chillies
30g/1oz chopped fresh parsley
1 egg
salt and pepper
a little plain flour
1 lime

Raita:
150mls/5fl oz natural yoghurt
30g/1oz chopped fresh mint (or 2 teaspoons mint sauce)
55g/2oz diced cucumber

Place the crabmeat, mashed potato, cooked long grain rice, parsley, 1 egg and a pinch of salt and pepper into a mixing bowl. Remove the stalk and cut the chillies in half lengthways. Scoop out and discard the seeds, finely chop the chillies and add to the mixture. Take care when handling chillies – either wear rubber gloves or be sure to thoroughly wash your hands to remove the fierce oils before they sting.

Shape into small patties, 25mm/2inches in diameter. You may need a light dusting of flour on your hands when doing this. Then deep fry in hot oil for 4–5 minutes. Remove when golden brown and sit them on kitchen paper for 30 seconds.

Raita is simple: just mix together the yoghurt, mint and cucumber and serve as a dip with the crab cakes. Serve with a wedge of lime and a small watercress salad.

Potted Salmon with Soursap

You may not have previously heard of soursap, but this is only a quaint colloquialism for sorrel – that fresh leafy herb that possesses a sour, somewhat citrus tang. It has long been used in Sorrel Sauce to accompany fish in classic French cuisine. This characterful herb goes just perfectly with salmon: so try this easy-to-make starter next time you have a dinner party.

For 6

340g/12oz fresh salmon
110g/4oz sorrel
splash of white wine
55g/2oz onion
a large pinch of ground nutmeg
110g/4oz of cream cheese
85g/3oz melted butter
1 teaspoon of horseradish sauce
1 lemon
6 sprigs of parsley
salt and pepper

Place the salmon in an ovenproof dish, drizzle a little white wine over the top, cover with foil and bake in a moderately hot oven preheated to 200°C/400°F/gas 6 for 12–15 minutes. Remove and allow to cool. Finally chop the onion and fry slowly in one third of the butter until soft. Add a pinch of nutmeg, the roughly chopped sorrel and cook until the leaves have started to break down, rather like cooked spinach. Remove from the heat and allow to cool. Place in the bowl of a food mixer the salmon, with all the bone and skin removed, cream cheese, horseradish, the remaining (melted) butter, and the juice of half the lemon. Then mix with the beater attachment on low speed until smooth. Taste and season with a little salt and pepper.

Take 6 ramekins and spoon a small amount of the salmon mixture into the bottom. Spread out evenly and then add quite a thin layer of soursap. Repeat layering thus until you reach the top of the ramekin, finishing with a layer of the salmon mixture. Slice the other half of the lemon and along with the sprigs of parsley garnish the ramekins. Refrigerate for at least one hour before serving with water biscuits or hot home-baked bread rolls.

Flora's Green Pigeon Pâté

This was of course named after the beautiful lawn, Flora's Green, which is surrounded by a stunning collection of rhododendrons here at Heligan. The local pigeon population also enjoys this area and while we were preparing the menu for one of our Feast Nights, Peter Stafford, the Managing Director, presented us with a dozen of these plump little fellows. Pigeon pâté was the result and I was most pleased with it!

For 8

4 pigeons (ask your butcher to remove all the bones leaving you with all the meat)
225g/8oz onion
4 cloves garlic
150mls/5fl oz red wine
225g/8oz chicken livers
small bunch of each of the following:
parsley, basil, thyme and rosemary
6 bay leaves
approx 570mls/1 pint chicken stock
1 tablespoon tomato purée
1 tablespoon olive oil
55g/2oz butter
salt and pepper

Firstly heat the oil in a large saucepan with a tightly fitting lid. Fry the pigeon flesh, chicken livers, onion and garlic for 5 minutes. Add the red wine, fresh herbs, bay leaves, tomato purée and a little salt and pepper. Pour in enough chicken stock to just cover the ingredients. Bring to the boil, giving everything a little stir. Simmer with the lid on as gently as you can – you may need to add more stock if it starts to dry up – you do not want too much liquid as this will affect the consistency of your pâté. Cooking this may take 1–2 hours depending on whether your pigeons were young or old and past-it! When the meat is tender remove from the heat and cool until a comfortable temperature to handle, then mince or whizz in a food processor.

Now you must taste and adjust the seasoning – at this stage the still quite liquid pate does not look very appetising, but never mind, taste it you must! Then spoon the mixture into a shallow earthenware dish, smooth out the surface, cover and chill in a refrigerator for 4 hours. By this time it should be quite set. To help stop discolouration, melt the butter and brush over the top. It is now ready to serve. Accompany this with beer bread (see recipe for Heligan Honey Ale Bread in A *Taste of Heligan – the best from the bakery*) and of course, Cornish butter!

Zingy Tomato Soup with Thai Spiced Beef

This is a tomato soup with a difference. The delicate strips of beef, marinated overnight, take on the most heavenly aroma when cooked. If you can resist eating them before they hit the soup all the better, the final touch being the fragrant fresh coriander. The humble tomato soup is given a new lease of life and is great served with prawn toast or even a few dim-sum on the side – whatever takes your fancy.

For 6

450g/1lb fresh tomatoes
110g/4oz carrots
110g/4oz onion
110g/4oz celery
1 litre/35fl oz vegetable stock
1 tablespoon tomato purée
1 tablespoon fresh chopped parsley
1 tablespoon fresh chopped lemon thyme
1 tablespoon fresh chopped coriander
salt and pepper

Beef:
170g/6oz rump steak cut into very thin strips
2 tablespoons olive oil
2 stalks of lemon grass
1 small green chilli (deseeded)
1 teaspoon paprika
1 spring onion, chopped

One day in advance, place the olive oil, lemon grass, paprika, spring onion and chilli in a liquidiser and whizz for 30 seconds. The resulting paste is then rubbed into the rump steak strips, which are covered and chilled in a refrigerator overnight.

The next day take a large saucepan, pour in the vegetable stock and then add the peeled and chopped carrot, onion and washed and chopped celery, parsley and thyme along with the tomato purée and bring to the boil. Then cut a cross in the top of each tomato, place in a sieve and pour a kettle of boiling water over the top. This will make the skins crack and peel very easily. Once peeled, roughly chop and add to the soup. Season with a little salt and pepper and simmer for one hour before whizzing in a liquidiser, returning to the pan, and placing on a low heat.

Heat a non-stick frying pan and fry the beef strips in the oil they are coated in, stirring occasionally, cooking for 10–12 minutes. When the beef is evenly brown, pour the soup into bowls, adding some spiced beef to each, followed by a generous sprinkle of coriander and serve.

Lobster Bisque

Killing lobsters… There are three schools of thought: firstly, the traditional 'drop them in a vat of boiling water' approach – with this method they do squeak a bit (only due to escaping air), which is rather off-putting. Secondly, advocated by many cooks, insert a sharp knife into a cross on the head then cut clean in half (which allegedly kills them instantly). Now our lobsters seem to be particularly lively and on using this method I find I can end up with 2 halves of lobster that are still equally lively. The third, and to my mind the best method, involves filling a pan with cold water, popping in the lobster and bringing to the boil, during which time the lobster seems to simply fall asleep. Far less stress for both lobster and cook!

For 4

675g/1lb 8oz lobster (live)
55g/2oz butter
2 tablespoons olive oil
1 onion, diced
half a lemon
2 tablespoons brandy
4 bay leaves
4 parsley stalks
1 large pinch ground nutmeg
1 litre/35fl oz fish stock
4 tablespoons double cream
55g/2oz plain flour
1 tablespoon chopped fresh parsley
salt and ground black pepper

Make sure the most generous portion goes to the person washing up – as there is an awful lot of it!

Fill a large pan with cold water, gently drop in the lobster, bring to the boil and simmer for 25 minutes. Remove the lobster and set aside to cool. When cool enough to handle, cut the lobster in half down the middle. Remove the meat from the lobster making sure you discard the little stomach sack from the head and the threadlike intestines. Dice the meat and set aside. Using a hammer, break up the shell and put in a clean saucepan along with the fish stock, nutmeg, parsley stalks, bay leaves and a little salt and pepper. Bring to the boil and simmer for 20 minutes. Drain this through a fine sieve into a jug. In a small frying pan, heat the olive oil, fry the onion for 5 minutes then add the lobster meat, brandy, the juice of half a lemon and the parsley, stir and cook for 3 minutes, then remove from heat.

In yet another clean saucepan, melt the butter, add the flour and cook for 4 minutes, stirring continuously. To this slowly add the fish stock, a drop at a time, stirring throughout to avoid lumps. When hot and of smooth consistency add the contents of your frying pan along with the double cream. Stir and heat through. When hot, taste and season with salt and pepper if necessary, and serve immediately with crusty French bread.

Spider Crab Chowder

Here in Cornwall we could not be better placed for getting hold of the freshest and by far the best seafood available. Our suppliers have their own boats and land their catches at nearby Fowey. If they have not caught the variety we require, then our fish may travel from Newlyn, Looe or Padstow. We usually have our sea food delivered live. You can't get any fresher than that! However spider crabs are often reluctant to go into a saucepan, and can spread themselves out to quite a diameter! So for this recipe I have left the cooking of the crab to the fishmonger, getting them in ready-done is much more user-friendly.

For 4-6

285g/10oz prepared spider crabmeat
the shell from the crabs
110g/4oz fish bones
(available from your fishmonger)
1 medium onion
1 stick of celery
55g/2oz butter
2 rashers smoked streaky bacon
170g/6oz peeled potatoes
1 litre/35fl oz water
150mls/5fl oz double cream
150mls/5fl oz milk
1 tablespoon fresh chopped thyme
4 bay leaves
1 tablespoon chopped fresh parsley
salt and pepper

Using a hammer roughly break up the crab shells, put in a saucepan with the fish bones and add the water. Bring to the boil and simmer for 30 minutes, before passing through a fine sieve into a clean pan. In a large soup pan melt the butter, finely dice the bacon and fry for 10 minutes, stirring to ensure even cooking. Wash and chop the celery, potato, onion and add to the bacon. Cook slowly for a further 10 minutes stirring frequently. Add the flour and stir for 2 minutes to cook out. Then, gradually pour on the stock from your crab shells, stirring continuously. Now add the thyme, parsley, milk, bay and a little salt and pepper, bring back to the boil and simmer for 15–20 minutes until your potatoes are cooked. Stir during cooking to prevent the soup from catching. When the potato is cooked, flake your crabmeat into the soup, stir in the double cream, heat through for a few minutes and serve immediately.

Great with fresh home-baked bread, and real butter!

Mutton and Winter Vegetable Soup

You may have a little trouble finding mutton these days, which is a pity. Many years ago mutton was more popular than lamb; but lamb, being less fatty and offering smaller, tender joints, is much more in line with today's consumer's wishes. Mutton if ripened by being well-hung and expertly trimmed and cut by a good butcher, can be excellent meat with a superb flavour. It's just during the last century that mutton has fallen out of favour, but I for one would like to see a revival. This soup is just the thing for a winter's day, especially if you have been working outside. Served with a hunk of fresh baked bread it's enough to warm any gardener all the way down to his boots!

For 4–6

225g/8oz finely diced leg of mutton (or lamb)
30g/1oz butter
1 onion
1 carrot
1 small parsnip
1 small potato
1 small leek
30g/1oz pearl barley
1 tablespoon chopped parsley
6 bay leaves
1litre/35fl oz good lamb or vegetable stock
salt and pepper
1 heaped tablespoon cornflour
60mls/2fl oz milk

Take a large saucepan and heat the butter, add to this the lamb and cook slowly for 10 minutes

Peel, wash and dice the parsnip, potatoes, leek and carrot. Add this to the pan and stir. Finely dice the onion and add to the pan along with the pearl barley, parsley and a little salt and pepper. Cook for 5 minutes stirring frequently, then pour in the stock. Bring to the boil, stir and gently simmer for one and a half hours with a tightly fitting lid and during this time top up with water if required.

Then carefully skim the excess fat from the top using a ladle. Mix the cornflour in with the milk and pour into the soup, stirring all the time. Season with a little salt and pepper to taste and simmer for a further 10 minutes before serving with freshly baked granary bread.

Scallops in Cornish Cider and Cream

Scallops are superb, succulent, fresh little medallions of flesh with endless possibilities, quick to cook and my favourite shellfish. Unfortunately, I am not the only one who thinks so. In the restaurant world there is such a thing, believe it or not, as a dish that is just too nice; when you produce a well balanced menu compiled of many great dishes full of colour varied in textures and tastes, only to find that almost every customer chooses the same dish – a rare occurrence but it does happen. This recipe is one such dish dominating a Feast Night evening here at Heligan. So if you cook this for a dinner party don't offer your guests an alternative as they won't want it and you will end up eating Boeuf Bourguignon for breakfast!

For 4

16–20 scallops, shelled
1 onion, very finely chopped
1 clove of garlic, crushed
150mls/5fl oz good dry white wine
120mls/4fl oz local cider, medium dry
180mls/6fl oz double cream
55g/2oz butter
1 tablespoon chopped fresh parsley
salt and pepper

and...
A CD of *Pêcheurs des Perles* by Bizet
(Act 1 scene IV – the duet)

Heap the butter in a large frying pan (one you can trust not to stick), add the scallops, sprinkle the onion and garlic around the scallops and cook for 2 minutes. Carefully turn them over, giving the onion a little stir as you do so and cook for a further 2 minutes.

Pour the cider over the scallops and bring to a rapid boil for a further 2 minutes, before adding the cream and stirring until it reaches a simmer. Add most of the parsley (saving a little to sprinkle over the finished dish).

Season to taste, stirring continuously. Serve, sprinkled with the rest of the chopped parsley and some choice, crisp, fresh vegetables. Pour yourself the white wine and listen to the *Pearl Fishers*, and of course eat the scallops! Can life get any better?

Megrim Sole Topped with Fresh Herbs

Megrim sole is another overlooked but exquisite fish from British waters. The fillets of flesh are normally quite thin, but for a few weeks a year around the middle of August they fatten up considerably. I was delighted to see such thick succulent fillets arrive at the kitchen and with such a fish it would be a shame to mask its flavour with a strong sauce, so I served this with dill butter just melting on the top of a fragrant herb breaded topping.

For 4

4 megrim sole fillets
110g/4oz butter
1 small bunch of each of the following: dill, parsley, lemon thyme, sweet marjoram and summer savory
3 slices of wholemeal bread
salt and pepper
1 lemon
4 sprigs of parsley for garnish

Place each fillet skin-side down on a lined greased baking sheet. Put the bread in a food processor and whizz to make bread crumbs. Put these in a bowl with a pinch of salt and pepper, then put all the herbs except the dill in the food processor and chop finely. Mix the herbs into the bread crumbs and spoon onto the top of the fillets, spreading out to cover the fish. Lightly pat the crumb down with your hand.

To make the dill butter, simply chop the dill and mix with the softened butter, shape into 4 small butter pats and chill in the fridge. To cook the fish only takes 10–15 minutes depending on the plumpness of the fish. Place them in a moderately hot oven 200°C/400°F/gas 6 until the bread crumbs are golden and the fish flesh is just cooked. Serve with the dill butter melting on the top. Garnish with a wedge of lemon and a sprig of parsley.

Lyonnaise potatoes go very well with this and to make them is very easy. You start with some hot sautéed potatoes, add a few fried onions and a good amount of chopped parsley, give them a light stir and they are ready to serve.

Lemon Thyme Lemon Sole

There are many varieties of thyme, both wild and cultivated. There is of course the common thyme, which is very useful, but also available are flavoured thymes with overtones of lemon, orange and even caraway. The best of these to my mind is lemon thyme – it goes wonderfully with fish and even just tucking a few sprigs under the skin imparts a subtle spicy lemon flavour. This particular dish sounds good and tastes great and it turned out to be very popular on Feast Nights.

For 4

4 x 225g/8oz fillets of lemon sole
20 sprigs of lemon thyme
55g/2oz melted butter
55g/2oz fresh bread crumbs
1 lemon
4 sprigs of flat parsley
salt and pepper

Rinse the lemon thyme and pluck the leaves from the stalks, mixing into the bread crumbs, along with a pinch of salt and pepper and the zest of half of the lemon (cut lengthways).

Arrange the fillets on a lightly greased baking tray, squeeze the juice from the zested half of the lemon, then evenly cover the top of each fish with the crumb mixture, patting down gently. Drizzle with melted butter and bake in a preheated oven 190°C/375°F/gas 5 for 15–20 minutes until golden brown.

Serve with the other half of the lemon cut into wedges and sprigs of parsley as garnish. The best thing to accompany this dish has got to be... chips! Not frozen ones, not baked in the oven; but real chips made from real potatoes cooked in a real chip pan! On this occasion you deserve it!

Skate Wings with Marjoram Butter and Samphire

Picking wild food can be full of surprises. I remember searching for two hours for mushrooms in Luxulyan woods once without any joy but then on returning to my car, what did I see but a spectacular crop of oyster mushrooms on a nearby tree. They looked just too good to be true, almost as though they were fresh from the supermarket shelves. If only I had noticed them two hours previously! Another thing – I have not had much luck with is samphire. I have read in books that it can be found along parts of the Cornish coast, but where? I just can't find it. So if anybody spots any I'd be glad to hear from you!

For 4

4 x 170g/6oz skate wing portions
110g/4oz rock samphire
1 tablespoon chopped fresh marjoram
55g/2oz softened butter
1 tablespoon olive oil
salt and cracked black pepper

Start by making the herb butter – mix the marjoram with the softened butter, form into a neat little pat on a piece of greaseproof paper and chill in the fridge.

Take your fish and arrange the pieces on a lightly greased baking tray, brush with olive oil and season with a little salt and cracked black pepper. Bake in a preheated oven 200°C/400°F/gas 6 for 12–15 minutes.

In the meantime put a small saucepan of water on to boil, wash your samphire in a colander and just before your fish is ready plunge the samphire into boiling water for no more than 1 minute.

To serve, carefully remove the fish with a fish slice onto 4 warmed plates, cut the marjoram butter into 4 equal portions and place one in the middle of each piece of fish. Drain your samphire and arrange in a neat pile on top of each fish. Serve immediately with some new potatoes and some honey-glazed carrots.

Fish

Black Bream Veronique

Black bream is another fish that is much underrated. With everybody wanting cod, plaice, sole or haddock, it is no wonder resources are running low. But there are countless more varieties of fish out there waiting to be tried. During my time at Heligan we have made a conscious effort to try new and exciting forms of fish. I have not yet regretted choosing any of them. Black bream was a great find. I just grilled the fillets for a few minutes and adapted a classical French dish normally associated with sole. It was an enormous success at one of our Feast Nights.

For 4

4 large fillets of black bream (or 8 small fillets)
90mls/3floz fish stock
60mls/2floz medium white wine
150mls/5floz double cream
1 teaspoon fresh chopped parsley
55g/2oz plain flour
55g/2oz butter
55g/2oz melted butter
1 lemon
about 20 seedless grapes
4 sprigs of fennel
salt and pepper

Start the sauce by boiling the fish stock and add white wine, parsley, a little salt and pepper and simmer for 5 minutes. Mix together the flour and butter to form a paste (this is called a beurre-manié and is mainly used for thickening fish sauces). Add this in small pieces to the simmering liquid, whisking all the time in order to avoid lumps. The sauce needs to be a little thicker than is normally required at this point. Cut the grapes in half and add half of these to the sauce, along with the cream. Give it a stir and put on a very low heat while you grill the fish.

Place the fish skin-side down on a greased baking tray lined with greaseproof paper. Brush with melted butter, season with a pinch of salt and pepper and place under a moderately hot grill for 4–8 minutes, depending on the size and thickness of your fish. When the fish is just cooked move to warm dinner plates and pour on some of the white wine sauce. Arrange the remaining grapes on top of this, followed by a sprig of fennel and a wedge of lemon.

Excellent served with some buttery new potatoes, and some stir-fried courgettes, peppers and button mushrooms.

Gurnard in Red Wine

Gurnard is hardly ever seen on restaurant menus, and recipes for it are few and far between, although it is quite popular in South America and some areas of Spain and Portugal. To my surprise a lot of our fishermen use gurnard as pot-bait. I just hope the lobsters appreciate it! If you ask your fishmonger to de-scale and fillet the fish for you, you will be left with two slender fillets of white flesh with a very colourful reddish skin. I was so pleased with the colour I decided to serve the fish with the sauce underneath. It just seemed a shame to hide this colourful fish.

For 4

4 x 110g/4oz gurnard or 8 fillets
110g/4oz butter
110g/4oz onion
1 clove of garlic
110g/4oz chopped fresh tomatoes
2 teaspoons of tomato purée
120mls/4fl oz of red wine
150mls/5fl oz of vegetable stock
small sprig of each of the following:
parsley, marjoram and thyme
4 large sprigs of fennel tops
1 heaped tablespoon cornflour
splash of water
salt and pepper
1 lemon

Firstly, make the sauce – melt half the butter in a saucepan and slowly cook off the onion (finely diced) and crushed garlic, until translucent and soft. Add the red wine and boil for a few minutes. Add the chopped tomatoes, tomato purée and vegetable stock and simmer for 20 minutes. Chop the herbs finely excluding the fennel and add to the sauce. Thicken the sauce by mixing together the cornflour and a little water, stirring to form a smooth paste, add a little more water until it resembles the consistency of double cream. Stir this into the simmering sauce, adding gradually until the sauce is sufficiently thickened. You may not need to add it all. Finally, season with salt and pepper to taste.

Now let's move on to the fish – lightly grease a baking sheet. On it place the fish skin-side down, melt the remaining butter and brush over the fish. Sprinkle with a pinch of salt and a twist of ground black pepper. Place in a preheated oven 190°C/375°F/gas for 10–12 minutes, or until the fish is just cooked. To serve, put a small puddle of the hot sauce on one half of a warmed plate. Place the fillets leaning against each other, standing on the sauce. Garnish with lemon and fennel. Ideal with buttery new potatoes and steamed vegetables.

Red Mullet with Gooseberry and Ginger Compôte

There are certain bumper crops at particular times of the year that can really tax one's culinary imagination. The gooseberry crop, though plentiful, is much easier to deal with than some, as gooseberries have great character and lend themselves to many dishes, even beyond the world of desserts and puddings. A gooseberry compôte pepped up with a little root ginger was just what I was looking for to accompany some red mullet. I thought this was quite an original idea, but have since found a recipe for mackerel cooked with gooseberries, so maybe it isn't so unusual to mix gooseberries with

For 4

4 red mullet (gutted and de-scaled)
225g/8oz gooseberries
2cm/1inch piece of root ginger
30g/1oz granulated sugar
55g/2oz butter
splash of water
1 lemon
4 sprigs of fennel or dill
some cracked sea salt and ground black pepper

Wash and remove the stalks from the gooseberries, put in a pan with a splash of water and the sugar and put on a low heat.

Peel and grate the ginger and add to the gooseberries, cover and leave to break down slowly, stirring occasionally. When this resembles a fruit compôte in consistency remove from the heat and allow to cool.

Place the fish on a greased baking sheet, brush with melted butter and sprinkle with a little sea salt and black pepper. Roast in a preheated oven 200°C/400°/gas 6 for 10–15 minutes, depending on the size of the fish.

Serve immediately with the gooseberry and ginger compôte, a wedge of lemon, and a sprig of fennel or dill.

Excellent accompanied by buttery new potatoes and lightly cooked seasonal fresh vegetables.

Turbot Baked with White Wine and Fennel

As a part-time angler myself, I am very appreciative of the superb specimens we get delivered to Heligan from our fishmonger: far larger and more impressive than anything I can catch! I am, however, not your normal angler, I don't enjoy sitting around all day not catching anything and I don't like battling with a big fish only to throw it back! The only reason I have for going fishing is to eat the fish! This is by far the most enjoyable part of the whole day. Either taken home and eaten for supper, or, cooked within minutes of landing on a little camping stove, with some butter and lemon. Throw it back? The very idea... This recipe uses turbot, a large flat fish similar to halibut but with a moist, more delicate flavoured flesh.

For 4

4 x 170g/6oz turbot fillets
1 large fennel bulb
2 tablespoons of olive oil
150mls/5fl oz medium dry white wine
salt and cracked black pepper
4 large sprigs of fennel tops
4 wedges of lemon

Wash and roughly cut the fennel bulb into 2cm/1inch pieces. Heat the oil in a large roasting tin and add the fennel. Roast in a preheated oven 190°C/375°F/gas 5 for 15 minutes. Remove from the oven and move the fennel pieces to one side of the tin.

Place the fish carefully in the roasting tin, pour white wine over the top and sprinkle with a little salt and cracked black pepper. Return to the oven for 15–20 minutes or until the fish is just cooked (do not overcook) – to test, insert a knife into the thickest part of the fish, parting the flakes and if the flesh still looks opaque then cook a little longer, but 15–20 minutes should be enough.

When cooked, remove from oven and serve on a warm plate with a few pieces of the roasted fennel bulb on top. Drizzle with some of the juices in the pan and finish with a large sprig of fennel draped over the fish, and a wedge of lemon on the side.

This dish goes well with new potatoes, roasted in their skins with fresh rosemary. Simple and delicious as all fish recipes should be.

Sirloin Braised with Cherries and Port

Despite having been a chef for many years I still have fond memories of being a butcher's assistant while at school. While my school chums were pounding the pavements delivering newspapers I was far better paid and had exciting jobs like plucking turkeys, gutting rabbits, boning out pigs' heads and making sausages. One old master butcher I have never forgotten about would drink a bottle of sherry every lunchtime, and wield razor sharp knives all afternoon – he had a very red nose but amazingly all fingers intact! The same old gent informed us that during wartime rationing the local butcher was the most eligible and hotly pursued bachelor around town – Rudolf Valentino would apparently not have stood a chance!

For 4

4 x 170g/6oz sirloin steaks
350g/12oz fresh cherries
425mls/15fl oz beef stock
1 small onion, diced
1 tablespoon sunflower oil
120mls/4fl oz port
30g/1oz plain flour
30g/1oz demerara sugar
salt and pepper
4 sprigs of fresh parsley

Heat the oil in a large flat pan that has a tight-fitting lid. Season the steaks with salt and pepper and fry for 3 minutes on both sides to seal, add the diced onion and cook for a further 3 minutes. Pour the stock over the steak and add the sugar and cherries (pitted). NB: keep back 4 perfect pairs of cherries for garnish. Cover with a tight-fitting lid and place in a preheated oven 200°C/400°F/gas 6 for 50–60 minutes.

Remove from the oven and place on a low heat on the hob, remove the lid with an oven glove, test with a knife and see if your meat is tender. If not, cook for a little longer. When tender remove the steaks and put on a plate in a warm oven.

Skim any fat from the top of the liquid – mix the flour and a splash of the port into a smooth paste before mixing in the remaining port. Use this to thicken the stock, stirring continuously to avoid lumps. Taste and season with a little salt and pepper. Pass through a sieve into a clean pan and keep on a low heat until required.

Serve the steaks with a covering of sauce and garnish with cherries and a sprig of parsley on each. Great served with the first new potatoes of the year and roasted vegetables.

Beef Stroganoff with Wild Mushroom Pilaff

Classical recipes used by chefs seem to fall into two categories: dishes which under no circumstances must be altered, or those which lend themselves to individual interpretation and regional variations. I have found stroganoff to fall into the latter category with every chef I have ever met doing a slightly different version and each vehemently believing his own recipe to be the best. It was this passion that once dropped me in hot water. While working alongside another chef in an Oxford restaurant I saw him add a large pinch of paprika – quite a common practice in itself but a little less than I would normally use, so, I reached for the pot of bright red powder and tipped a healthy heap into his bubbling pan; but on replacing the pot I realised it was in fact chilli powder! The dish was ruined, the chef was furious and I learned two valuable lessons: too many cooks spoil the broth and always read the label!

For 4–6

For Pilaff:
425mls/15fl oz long grain rice
425mls/15fl oz vegetable stock
110g/4oz assorted wild mushrooms
55g/2oz butter
55g/2oz diced onion
1 tablespoon chopped fresh parsley
salt and pepper

For Stroganoff:
675g/1lb 8oz tail end of beef fillet (cut into thin strips)
2 tablespoons olive oil
110g/4oz finely diced onion
2 tablespoons chopped parsley
1 teaspoon French mustard
2 tablespoons brandy
425mls/10fl oz double cream
1 tablespoon sweet paprika
salt and pepper
4–6 large sprigs of flat parsley

Starting with the pilaff – melt the butter in a thick metal roasting dish on the hob. Add the diced onion and cook without colour for 4 minutes, slice the mushrooms and add to the pan, along with the parsley, a little salt and pepper and the rice. Stir until the rice is evenly mixed and shining from the butter. Heat the vegetable stock until boiling and add to the rice. Foil over tightly and bake in a preheated oven 180°C/350°F/gas 4 for 35–40 minutes until the rice is tender and all liquid has been absorbed. When cooked leave covered in a very low oven until the stroganoff is ready to serve.

Now for the beef stroganoff – heat the oil in a large sauté pan over a fierce heat. Add the beef, stir fry for 2 minutes then add the diced onion, and fry for a further 4 minutes. Add the brandy, and flambé by tilting the pan towards the gas flame or carefully light with a taper. Turn down the heat and stir in the mustard and paprika, cook for a further 2 minutes, stir in the double cream and simmer for 4–5 minutes before finally adding the parsley and a little salt and pepper to taste. Serve on a bed of pilaff, garnished with a large sprig of flat parsley on the top.

Boeuf en Croûte

This classic dish is one that was not made at Heligan for the first few years of my being here because fillet steak is somewhat expensive. This changed when the first Heligan-reared beef appeared in my kitchen. Literally a whole ton of it! So for the first time every conceivable cut of beef was at my disposal. Boeuf en Croûte was always popular in restaurants where I had worked in the past and our Feast Nights were no exception.

For 4

4 x 140g/5oz fillet steaks
340g/12oz ready-to-roll puff pastry
1 teaspoon of English mustard
30g/1oz beef dripping
110g/4oz good quality pâté
1 beaten egg
salt and pepper
dusting of plain flour
a little water

Trim any sinew from around the fillet steaks, season well with salt and pepper on both sides. Heat the dripping in a frying pan and when hot fry the steaks on both sides for 2 minutes to seal them. Remove from the pan and allow to cool completely.

Now take your puff pastry, cut into 4 equal squares and roll out on a floured table into an oblong, each slightly larger than twice the size of a steak. Place a 30g/1oz slice of pâté in the middle of each square of pastry, on top of this goes a fillet steak, spread with a little English mustard. Brush around the outside edge of the pastry with water and lift the pastry over the top to form a parcel, pushing the edges together and neatly crimp. Pierce the middle with the point of a small knife and brush with beaten egg. Repeat this for all four steaks. Place these on a lightly greased baking tray and bake in a preheated oven 200°C/400°F/gas 6 for 20–25 minutes until golden brown. Serve immediately. Personally I think a rich gravy with a good dash of port would complement this beautifully.

If you are preparing for a dinner party you can do all the hard work in advance, chill in a fridge thus leaving only the final baking to do at the last minute.

Braised Beef with MacGregor's Favourite Beetroot

No, 'MacGregor' is not one of our gardeners, but MacGregor's Favourite is one of the many varieties of beetroot grown at Heligan. This is a hearty warming dish that takes on a rich, deep, red colour. When we made this for one of our Feast Nights we used beef reared by one of our farming neighbours on the Tremayne Estate. I honestly think that was the best beef I have ever eaten – so good in fact that we went on to order half a cow.

For 4–6

675g/1lb 8oz diced braising steak
170g/6oz diced onion
225g/8oz of beetroot (if you can't get MacGregor's Favourite, his 2nd favourite will do!)
1 tablespoon sunflower oil
570mls/1 pint of beef stock
150mls/5 fluid oz red wine
85g/3oz plain flour
5 bay leaves
55g/2 oz sliced mushrooms
small sprig of each of the following: parsley, marjoram and thyme
salt and pepper

Firstly boil the beetroot until tender, remove the skin and dice into half inch cubes. Then heat the oil in a large saucepan and fry the meat until evenly sealed. Add the onion and bay leaves and then cook for another 5 minutes. Chop the herbs and add them to the beef along with the wine and beef stock. Bring to the boil, put a lid on the pan and simmer gently for one hour. Then add the mushrooms and cook for a further 10 minutes. At this point carefully taste a cube of beef, if it is tender, add the beetroot and cook for a further 5 minutes. If it is not tender, then simmer for a while longer and then add the beetroot. It is important to stir this dish now and again throughout cooking and maybe add a splash of water if it starts to reduce too much. Finally, mix the flour with a little water making it into a smooth paste, then add a little more water until it resembles the consistency of double cream. This is what we call in the trade 'a slake'; add this to the beef stirring all the time until it thickens the desired amount. The amount of slake you require may vary, so do this gradually. Taste and adjust seasoning if required, and serve.

This casserole is great in the autumn served with Champ (mashed potato with butter and chopped spring onions/scallions – a traditional Irish dish).

Beef, Barley and Real Ale Pie

There is nothing more heart-warming on a dismal winter day than the thought of hot wholesome food awaiting your return home. I often plan my cooking around walking the dog – slow cooked lamb stew would give us enough time for a long walk along the cliff path – a pie such as this will give a brisk 30 minute walk through the woods – it all depends on a) the cut of meat, b) the inclemency of the weather and c) the enthusiasm of the bull terrier at the end of the lead. As long as she gets a share of the pie, canine contentment is assured.

For 4–6

Filling:
675g/1lb 8oz of diced chuck steak
30g/1oz beef dripping
1 onion, finely chopped
110g/4oz button mushrooms
425mls/15fl oz good beef stock
5 drops of Worcester sauce
6 bay leaves
55g/2oz pearl barley
1 tablespoon chopped parsley
30g/1oz cornflour
salt and pepper
a little cold water

Pastry:
450g/16oz plain flour
225g/8oz butter
approx 6 tablespoons cold water
pinch of salt
1 beaten egg

Heat the dripping in a large saucepan, add the beef and fry for 15 minutes until all meat is evenly sealed. Add the diced onion, mushrooms, pearl barley and cook for a few minutes. Pour on the beef stock, add the Worcester sauce, bring to the boil and simmer for at least an hour, or until your meat is just tender. Thicken with cornflour mixed with a splash of cold water, stirring continuously as you add to the hot mixture. Taste and correct the seasoning. Set aside to cool.

Using your fingertips, rub the butter into the sifted flour and salt until you have an even sandy texture. Add 4 tablespoons of cold water and work into a paste. If it feels a little tight, add a little more water, wrap in cling film, and chill for 30 minutes. Grease a large 30cms/12 inch round pie dish, roll out half the pastry to the thickness of a pound coin. Lift the pastry onto your dish, tuck into the corners, trim off any excess pastry and brush the rim with water.

Using a slotted spoon, remove all the meat and mushrooms, spreading evenly in the pastry base. Pour the sauce over the top until just below the rim of your dish. Save the remaining sauce to serve with your pie later. Roll the second piece of pastry and lay it on the top of the pie, lightly press down around the edge and trim off any excess pastry. Crimp all around the edge. Brush with beaten egg and pierce the centre with a knife. Bake in a preheated oven 180°C/350°F/gas 4 for 40–45 minutes until golden brown. Great served with fluffy mashed potato and Savoy cabbage!

Steak and Oyster Pudding

This is a classy alternative to the equally delicious Steak and Kidney Pudding. I have also seen this done with mussels but oysters to my mind can't be beaten! If you have any difficulty opening oysters just ask your fishmonger to remove them from their shells. They are normally quite pleased to do this – it's only when, like me, you ask them to do three hundred you may then sense a little resistance!

For 4

675g/1lb 8oz of diced chuck steak
8 oysters
1 onion, finely chopped
570mls/1 pint good beef stock
1 tablespoon chopped fresh parsley
55g/2oz plain flour
salt and pepper

Pastry:
450g/1lb self raising flour
225g/8oz shredded beef suet
5–6 tablespoons cold water
pinch of salt and a little butter

Start by making the pastry. Sift the flour and salt into a mixing bowl, stir in the suet and then add enough water to form a soft dough, stirring as you go. Place three quarters of the mix on a floured table, dust well with flour and roll out to 1cm/half an inch thickness – large enough to line a 1kg/2lb 4oz pudding basin.

Grease the basin with a little butter and carefully line with the rolled out suet crust pastry. Trim off excess pastry but leave 1cm/half an inch hanging over the edge. Place the shelled oysters in the bottom and sprinkle the parsley over them, then roll the diced beef and onions in the flour and put this on top of the oysters, season with a little salt and pepper and then pour over enough stock to come two thirds up the bowl.

Roll out the remaining pastry and place this on the top of your meat, wet around the edge with water and bring the edges together, pressing to form a seal. Cover with a disc of greaseproof and then tinfoil, tie with string around the rim of the basin (if you have a pleat in your greaseproof and tinfoil this will allow for expansion).

Place your pudding in a large saucepan and half fill with water. Bring to the boil and simmer for 4–5 hours. Keep covered with a tight-fitting lid and top up with water during cooking. When cooked, turn out carefully onto a serving dish, cut at the table and serve with buttery potatoes, baby carrots and a good rich gravy.

Pan Fried Lamb with Lemon and Juniper

Lamb cooked this way should be served as you would a steak, but in this case you are offering your guests something much more: lamb marinated for a full two days with the fresh zestiness of lemon and the distinctive, pungent, floral overtones of the juniper just singing on your tongue. Exceptionally simple to cook, it's well worth the 2-day wait. Juniper is best known as the berry used to flavour gin but that is not all. It is said to be very beneficial to health. Historical physicians claim it to be 'excellent against the biting of venomous beasts', 'a sure-fire cure for falling sickness and dropsy' and guaranteed to 'stay all fluxes' – isn't medical science a marvellous thing!

For 4

4 x 225g/8oz lean lamb leg steaks
1 lemon
2 tablespoons of olive oil
12 juniper berries
salt and cracked black pepper

Take each steak and trim any excess fat from around the outside. Lay the steaks on a sturdy surface and tenderise with a meat mallet or rolling pin – do this on both sides. Then, crush your juniper berries with a mortar and pestle and mix with the olive oil in a small jug – adding to this the juice and zest of the lemon and a good pinch of salt and pepper. Put the steaks into a large mixing bowl and pour the lemon and juniper mixture over the top. Rub in well so that every part of the lamb is coated, cover with cling film and refrigerate for two days.

To cook, simply heat a non-stick frying pan or a cast iron pan (well-seasoned) now fry your steaks in the oil they are coated in for 8–10 minutes on both sides, less if you prefer your lamb a bit pinker inside. Serve immediately with mushrooms, grilled tomatoes and sautéed potatoes or alternatively some couscous or Bulgar wheat would work well.

Of course you don't have to fry them – these steaks could also be cooked under a hot grill or even on a barbecue.

Noisettes of Lamb, Studded with Rosemary and Garlic

Many people appreciate the succulent, tender and almost sweet flavour of English lamb. But the close relationship we have with our neighbouring farmers enables us to use the best lamb Cornwall has to offer. In the spring we have the lambs delivered whole and butcher them ourselves, this way the cuts of meat best suit our requirements. Cornish lamb paired with our fresh rosemary, a hint of garlic and served with a roast gravy infused with fresh mint gives you a Sunday roast with a difference.

For 4

2 noisettes of lamb (best end of neck, boned and rolled)
6 cloves of garlic
20 sprigs of fresh rosemary
2 tablespoons of sunflower oil
570mls/1 pint of lamb stock
1 tablespoon of cornflour
2 tablespoons of fresh mint sauce
salt and black pepper

Heat the oil in a large frying pan and when very hot, place the noisettes in the pan to seal them. Make sure you turn them so they lightly brown evenly, not forgetting both ends of the two rolled joints. When thoroughly sealed, remove from the heat and leave to cool. Peel the garlic and slice into pointed slivers to resemble a flaked almond. Cut the rosemary into very small sprigs, about 2cm/1inch in length, then with a small sharp knife make small incisions through the skin of the lamb inserting a sliver of garlic in one cut, followed by a sprig of rosemary in the next. Continue this process until both joints are evenly studded. Place the joints in a roasting tin, sprinkle with salt and freshly ground black pepper. Roast in a preheated oven 220°C/425°F/gas 7 for 20–25 minutes. The very centre of the meat should still be pink, but if you prefer you may cook the lamb a little longer at 150°C/300°F/gas 2 for 5–10 minutes. However, slightly pink is by far the better tasting meat and very tender.

When the lamb is cooked remove from the oven and stand for 5 minutes to relax. Then carve into 2cm/1inch thick roundels allowing 3 per portion. Serve with a mint gravy made by thickening the heated stock with a slake made from cornflour and a little water. When you are happy with the thickness add the mint sauce, stir and season to taste. Pour over the lamb and garnish with sprigs of rosemary. To accompany this I would recommend roasted potatoes with a light dusting of paprika and one of the first spring vegetables: purple sprouting broccoli.

Lamb

Spiced Lamb Kebabs with Jewelled Couscous

In the A Taste of Heligan *recipe books, you will often read of Heligan's fresh produce, the wild mushrooms and herbs, and now of the wonderful meat reared on the estate, all of which for a chef are a delight to use. However, this is not all that we produce at Heligan – for instance our Whole-Tree Policy means that when a tree is felled, every single part is used; the wood is cut and seasoned for use on the estate, a mulch is also produced and used throughout the gardens; but the best part for me is the Heligan charcoal. It lights and cooks like no other. This lamb dish is a great example of what barbecue food should be like.*

For 4

Kebabs:
675g/1lb 8oz lamb leg steak – diced
2 red onions
4 tablespoons olive oil
2 teaspoons soy sauce
3 teaspoons demerara sugar
4 teaspoons garam masala
2 teaspoons ground fenugreek
1 lemon – juice and zest

Couscous:
170g/6oz couscous
345mls/12fl oz hot vegetable stock
2 tablespoons olive oil
1 red pepper, diced
1 green pepper, diced
2 spring onions, chopped
1 lemon – juice and zest
2 tablespoons chopped, fresh parsley
salt and pepper

Starting with the lamb – a full 24 hours in advance of cooking – mix together the olive oil, soy sauce, demerara sugar, garam masala, fenugreek, and the juice and zest of the lemon. Place the lamb in a large bowl and pour the marinade over the top. Give a good stir, cover with cling film and chill overnight in a fridge. The following day, peel the red onions and cut into 2cm/1inch chunks. If you leave as much of the root end on as possible, this tends to hold the layers together. Take your lamb and onion pieces and arrange them evenly shared between 4 metal skewers. Cook over a hot barbecue for 15–20 minutes, turning frequently. You may also cook them under a grill in a similar manner. Serve piping hot with the couscous.

To make the couscous, heat the vegetable stock, place the couscous in a large bowl, cover with the stock and soak for 10 minutes or until all the liquid has been absorbed. In a large frying pan heat the olive oil, add the peppers and onions and gently fry for 5 minutes. When the couscous is ready add this to the pan along with the lemon juice and zest. Stir carefully for one minute, remove from the heat and fold in the fresh chopped parsley. Season to taste with salt and pepper and serve with the lamb kebabs.

A nice accompaniment to go with this would be to roast some cherry tomatoes with olive oil, black olives and basil for 8–10 minutes – simple but delicious!

Shank of Lamb in Red Wine and Redcurrants

This quite humble cut of lamb seems to be enjoying a revival over the last five years, popping up on menus all the time. Although this cut needs long, slow cooking it is well worth the wait. The meat becomes so sweet and tender and when cooked with red wine and redcurrants forms a delicious sauce that seems to cling to the meat. Our chef Simon tasted this dish (as every conscientious chef should) – however, he did go on to eat three portions that night – he's nothing if not thorough!

For 4

4 shanks of lamb
1 onion
110g/4oz fresh redcurrants
3 tablespoons redcurrant jelly
570mls/1 pint lamb stock
150mls/5fl oz red wine
4 bay leaves
1 tablespoon of cornflour (if required)
a little water
salt and pepper

In a large sturdy roasting tin place your lamb with the bones pointing upwards. Finely dice the onion and scatter around the lamb along with the bay leaves. In a saucepan, warm up the redcurrant jelly, adding the wine and stock, bring to the boil and pour over the lamb. Pluck the redcurrants from their stalks but leave 4 of the best strings of redcurrants for garnish later. Drop the plucked redcurrants into the roasting tin, cover with foil and roast in a preheated oven 180°C/350°F/gas 4 for 2–3 hours. During this time keep an eye on the liquid – if it evaporates too much top up with water. When the lamb is very tender, carefully lift the shanks from the tin using a fish slice (you don't want the meat to come away from the bones). Place these on a plate in a low oven to keep warm. Put the roasting tin with the liquid onto the hob and simmer. Using a ladle, skim as much fat from the surface of the liquid as you can, then if sauce is not thick enough, thicken with cornflour mixed with water gradually added to your sauce, stirring continuously until the right consistency is achieved. At this point I prefer to pass the sauce through a sieve to give a smooth finish, but you could of course use it as it is – taste and season with salt and pepper if required.

Move the lamb on to 4 warm plates and coat with sauce. Garnish with your 4 strings of redcurrants and serve with saffron potatoes and fresh vegetables. To make the saffron roast potatoes: boil your potatoes first for 10 minutes in water infused with saffron. Then roast in the normal manner. They taste and smell superb and take on a golden glow.

Curried Lamb with Almonds and Cream

Britain is without doubt a nation of curry lovers. In the last half a century it has overtaken all other foods in the popularity steaks. When cooked well, with a delicate balance of distinctive spices, it can be a joy to eat. A good curry does not have to blow your head off. It should instead tease and excite your palate, taking you on a culinary journey. This truly is food for the soul. This recipe uses almonds, not only for their creamy flavour, but also to thicken the sauce itself and, with very little chilli, it allows you to taste the character of each spice individually.

For 4

675g/1lb 8oz lean diced lamb
30g/1oz butter
1 tablespoon sunflower oil
2 onions, finely diced
2 cloves of garlic
1 tablespoon mango chutney
1 teaspoon turmeric
2 teaspoons ground coriander
2 teaspoons ground cumin
1 teaspoon black mustard seeds
1 teaspoon ground fenugreek
large pinch chilli powder
570mls/1pint lamb stock
2 heaped tablespoons ground almonds
1 tablespoons toasted flaked almonds
1 small bunch coriander leaves
150mls/5fl oz single cream

Start by heating the butter and oil in a large saucepan. Fry the lamb for 10 minutes stirring to ensure even cooking. Add to this the onion, turmeric, ground coriander, cumin, mustard seeds, fenugreek and chilli powder, stir thoroughly. Crush the garlic and add to the pan along with the mango chutney, stir and cook gently for 5 minutes, then pour on the chicken stock, bring to the boil and simmer for 35–40 minutes.

When the lamb is tender add the ground almonds and simmer for 10–15 minutes, stirring occasionally (the ground almonds will slowly thicken the sauce as they cook out). When sauce has thickened stir in the cream and heat through. Finally serve with the toasted almonds and coarsely chopped coriander leaves on the top.

To accompany this only basmati rice will do!

Minted Lamb and Butter Bean Casserole

Until I arrived at Heligan, pulses and beans had never generated much culinary excitement – in the restaurant kitchen I trained in, bags of lentils would sit sadly at the back of the store room only to eventually be used up in a soup. But here things are different – the most obvious difference being the unusual varieties we grow here; you just cannot buy them anywhere else. The colourful variations and patterns always amaze me. And the names sound so good on the menu: Lazywife, Cowboy Pony and Two-colour Cocoa, but the two varieties I love best are: Soldier Beans (each one has a little soldier standing to attention on the skin) and Killer Whale Beans (half black/half white with a little blow-hole marked on its head)! I am making this recipe with butter beans, as you'll have no trouble finding them and they go so well with the minted lamb.

For 4

675g/1lb 8oz diced braising lamb
1 onion
1 carrot
1 (400g) tin of butter beans
110g/4oz mushrooms
1 bunch fresh mint
570mls/1pint hot lamb stock
mint sauce
1 heaped tablespoon cornflour
a little water
salt and pepper

In an ovenproof casserole dish with a tight-fitting lid place the lamb, mint sauce, stock and a little salt and pepper. Peel and dice the carrot and onion adding these to the casserole, slice the mushrooms and chop the mint and add these also. Give a brief stir, replace lid, and cook slowly in a pre-heated oven 170°C/325°F/gas 3 for 2 hours, during which you may wish to top up with water if the liquid evaporates too much.

Remove from the oven, skim any excess fat off with a ladle, add the drained and rinsed butter beans and return to the oven for a further 30 minutes.

After 30 minutes, mix the cornflour with a little water and pour into the casserole, stirring continuously to avoid lumps. Return to the oven for 5 minutes to cook out the cornflour, season to taste with salt and pepper and serve.

I think the perfect potato dish to serve with this would be 'champ' – an Irish dish of mashed potatoes with spring onions. The recipe for this you will find in A *Taste of Heligan – vegetarian and fruit recipes*.

Pork and Bramley Apple Parcels

Tenderloin is quite simply the 'fillet steak' of pork – tender fillets without any fat or gristle. Ideal if the dish you are making requires a short cooking time. It's great for stir-fries and when cut into medallions and pan-fried it is ready in minutes. For this recipe it's just perfect. By the time the pork is cooked, the filo pastry is crisp and golden brown. To accompany this the sauce has a fruity quality with just a hint of spice.

For 4

Parcels:
4 x 110g/4oz pieces of tenderloin of pork
1 Bramley apple
12 squares of filo pastry
55g/2oz butter
2 tablespoons sunflower oil
salt and pepper

Sauce:
290mls/10fl oz chicken stock
150mls/5fl oz apple juice
1 tablespoon sugar
large pinch of ground cinnamon
large pinch of ground nutmeg
1 tablespoon cornflour
a little water
salt and pepper

Peel and core the cooking apple, cutting four 5mm/quarter inch wedges and dice the rest. Cut each piece of pork almost in half lengthways, open up the cut and put a wedge of apple in each. Neatly close again. Then on a board, pile up 3 squares of filo pastry, each one slightly offset to the one underneath. Lightly brush each layer with water to stick them together. Do this 4 times and place in the centre of each a piece of pork. Gather the pastry in a bunch encasing the pork, pinching the top to secure each parcel. Place on a lightly greased baking sheet. Melt the butter and liberally brush over your parcels. Bake these in a pre-heated oven 190°C/375°F/gas 5 for 30–35 minutes.

Now for the sauce, place the rest of the apple which you have diced in a saucepan, bring gently to the boil and simmer until the apple is soft. Then add the chicken stock, nutmeg and cinnamon, bring to the boil and thicken with cornflour mixed with a little water. Pour this into your sauce gradually, stirring continuously to avoid lumps. Then simmer for 2 minutes, taste and season with salt and pepper.

To serve, pour a puddle of sauce directly onto the plate, placing a pork parcel into the centre. Ideal served with some stir-fried vegetables.

Home Grown Toad-in-the-Hole

Just as a point of interest, I am actually cooking this as I write and by the end of this recipe I will be eating this somewhat traditional British dish. However, this is no ordinary toad-in-the-hole because I am now using the very first sausages made from our own pigs. This has taken hours of picking the fresh herbs, and many more hours involving the butcher in the neighbouring farm shop turning our pigs into the superb sausages I am cooking now. George, the butcher, showed great resolve in managing not to drink any of the gallons of real ale I provided him with, and subsequently produced 1400 Heligan pork, real ale and rosemary sausages. Although these are only available to us chefs at Heligan I am sure a visit to your local butcher will provide you with interesting regional varieties.

For 4

8 Heligan pork, real ale and rosemary sausages or
any good quality butcher's sausages
110g/4oz plain flour
1 large egg
290mls/10fl oz milk
pinch of salt
30g/1oz dripping or oil

Starting with the Yorkshire pudding mix, sift the flour and salt into a basin, make a well in the centre, break in the egg and half the milk, whisk into a smooth texture, gradually adding the rest of the milk before allowing the mixture to rest for half an hour.

Heat the dripping in a roasting pan and add the sausages, place in a preheated oven 220°C/425°F/gas 7 for 5–8 minutes until the oil is smoking – remove from the oven, close the oven door behind you as you don't want to lose that heat – pour the Yorkshire pudding mix over the sausages and return to the oven, turning up the heat to 240°C/450°F/gas 8 for 10 minutes, then turn back down to 220°C/425°F/gas 7 for a further 20 minutes. Should the batter that has risen start to brown a little too much, gradually turn the oven down a few degrees at a time. When your Yorkshire has set in the centre and is golden brown around the edges it is ready to serve.

A nice rich gravy should accompany this along with mashed parsnips and potatoes and some winter vegetables.

Pork

Marsala Pork with Kiwi Salsa

I must say I haven't seen kiwi fruit growing at Heligan – the original male plant in the Italian Garden has not taken to the new female we offered, however, many of the other ingredients in the salsa were home-grown, such as the chillies, onions, tomatoes, garlic and fresh herbs. The kiwi's flavour although quite sweet, is backed up by a lot of acidity. This often clashes with other ingredients and can alter their flavour, but in this case the robust spicy salsa keeps the kiwi in its place and goes well with a slightly sweet Marsala sauce.

For 4

4 pork steaks
290mls/10fl oz of chicken stock
120mls/4fl oz of Marsala wine (Moscatel can be used)
30g/1oz cornflour
splash of water
1 tablespoon of olive oil
few splashes of Worcestershire sauce
1 tablespoon of demerara sugar
2 kiwi fruit
1 red pepper
4 tomatoes
55g/2 oz onion
2 cloves of garlic
3 red or green chillies
sprigs of parsley, oregano and coriander
30mls/1fl oz of tomato ketchup
salt and pepper

For the salsa, place the de-seeded red pepper, roughly chopped tomatoes, diced onion, skinned garlic cloves, whole chillies with the stalk removed (remove the seeds for a less fierce salsa), all the herbs, the tomato ketchup and a large pinch of salt in a food processor, then whizz until quite smooth. Peel and cut the kiwi into a small dice, stir into the salsa and put to one side.

For the sauce, heat the stock and the wine together in a pan, bring to the boil and thicken with a slake made from cornflour and a little water, taste and season with salt and pepper and keep on a low heat.

Brush pork steaks with olive oil, a few splashes of Worcestershire sauce and a light sprinkling of demerara sugar and place on a greased baking tray. Roast in a preheated moderately hot oven at 200°C/400°F/gas 6, for 20–30 minutes, depending on the cut and thickness of your steaks. For the lesser quality cuts of meat I recommend adding a splash of stock and covering with foil before cooking at a slightly lower temperature for at least 45–60 minutes. When your pork is tender, serve with a covering of Marsala sauce and side helping of kiwi salsa.

Fondant potatoes and honey roast vegetables go very well with this dish. To make fondant potatoes, place some peeled, raw, potatoes cut to even sizes in a roasting pan and half cover with stock, season and roast in a hot oven, turning them a few times until golden brown and all the stock is absorbed into the potatoes. These are remarkably similar to roast potatoes but virtually the same calories as boiled potatoes.

Pork and Scrumpy Cobbler

There are so many good things about this dish - prime, locally reared pork, fresh cooking apples with an unmistakable smell of autumn and of course the potent, Cornish Scrumpy – always buy more than you need for this recipe – as rest assured it won't go to waste! But for me the best thing has got to be 'the dumpling' – the perfect comfort food as the autumn nights close in. I just can't resist them. But who cooks the very best dumplings? Fortunately for me my wife Angela seems to have this down to a fine art. Her dumplings are truly magnificent.

For 4

675g/1lb 8oz lean diced pork
2 tablespoons sunflower oil
2 onions
2 cooking apples
290mls/10fl oz Scrumpy
290mls/10fl oz chicken stock
1 tablespoon fresh chopped parsley
2 teaspoons sugar
1 tablespoon cornflour
a little water
salt and pepper

Dumplings:
225g/8oz self raising flour
110g/4oz beef suet
approximately 5 tablespoons cold water
pinch of salt

In a metal casserole dish (cast iron is best) heat the oil and fry the pork for 10 minutes stirring to ensure even cooking. Peel and dice the onion and cooking apples, adding them to the pan. Give another little stir then pour in the cider and stock, seasoning with a little salt and pepper. Stir in the sugar and parsley, cover with a tight-fitting lid and cook in a preheated oven 200°C/400°F/gas 6 for 1 hour 30 minutes. During this time check the liquid for evaporation and top up with a splash of water if required. Remove from the oven and put back on the hob, skim any excess fat from the top with a ladle and thicken by adding the cornflour mixed with some water. Pour this in gradually and stir continuously to avoid lumps. Taste and season with salt and pepper if required.

Now on to the dumplings... Sift the flour and salt into a mixing bowl, add the suet and mix in with a spoon. Make a well in the centre and add the water gradually, stirring all the time to form a soft dough (you may not need all the water) – flour your hands and divide the dough into four – shape into even sized balls and place them on the top of your pork. Replace the lid and return to the oven for 25–30 minutes at a lower temperature of 180°C/350°/gas 4. Test a dumpling by inserting a small knife – if it comes out clean then it's done. This is a meal in itself and the only thing to serve with it is a side order of more dumplings and a glass of red wine!

Loin of Pork stuffed with Bramble and Quince

Since our first pork arrived at the Heligan kitchen several years ago we have created many different recipes drawing on influences from home and abroad, but you just can't beat roast pork with crackling and apple sauce. Simple, but why complicate things when it tastes so good! At Heligan we once spit roasted four pigs for a large function. This involved four chefs, starting at 6am, basting for six hours, and carving for two hours. This recipe is not quite so labour intensive – developed for our Christmas Feast Nights we used Heligan pork, home grown quinces and blackberries from hedgerows on the estate.

For 6–8

2.3kgs/5lb loin of pork, boned (but not rolled)
1 onion
55g/2oz butter
225g/8oz blackberries
2 quinces, peeled and grated
55g/2oz sugar
285g/10oz fresh bread crumbs
1 egg
2 tablespoons sunflower oil
4–5 metres strong cotton parcel string

Place your loin of pork on a cutting board and score the skin with the point of a sharp knife in diagonal lines 2cms/1 inch apart – turn the joint and lie skin-side down and with a sharp knife cut along the underside of the eye of the meat (this is the large lean piece of meat which becomes the 'eye' of a pork chop). Cut out the eye but leave attached by the bottom 2cms/1 inch. Fold this over to one side ready for stuffing.

To make the stuffing, melt the butter in a saucepan and gently fry the onions until soft. In a separate saucepan heat the blackberries and quince and cook gently until the juice has come out of the blackberries and is bubbling. Simmer for 5 minutes stirring continuously before pushing through a sieve into a mixing bowl. Add your onions, bread crumbs, sugar, a little salt and pepper and finally the egg. Stir thoroughly (you may need to use a few more bread crumbs – all depending on how juicy your blackberries were). When a stuffing-like consistency has been reached, evenly spread the stuffing over the loin of pork. Carefully fold back the 'eye' of the meat and roll from the thick end. When a good shape is formed tie with string at 2cms/1 inch intervals along the loin. Rub the oil into the skin and liberally sprinkle with salt. Place in a roasting tin with a little water in the bottom and start cooking in a preheated oven 220°C/425°F/gas 7 for 30 minutes then reduce the heat to 190°C/375°F/gas 5 for a further 2hrs–2hrs 30 minutes. Test by inserting a knife into the centre of the joint. If the juices run clear then it is cooked. If not, return to the oven for a little longer.

When cooked, remove the joint and rest for 5 minutes before carving. This is easier if you remove the crackling first then slice the joint thickly. Make a gravy in the usual way using the meat juices and serve with apple sauce, roast potatoes and your favourite vegetables.

Christmas Spiced Honey-Roast Ham

This is an amazingly simple recipe to prepare, but it does, however, depend upon two crucial factors. Firstly, do you have a saucepan large enough to cook a piece of gammon this size? And secondly, can you gather enough people to eat a piece of meat this size? Christmas is of course the perfect time for this but a summer garden party is an equally good opportunity to cook this cold-cut which everyone will rave about.

For 12+

1 large green gammon (boned, but with the knuckle left on)
2 onions
10 bay leaves
20 peppercorns
40 cloves
2 teaspoons ground cinnamon
2 teaspoons ground nutmeg
large pinch ground ginger
110g/4oz demerara sugar
225g/8oz clear honey
handful of parsley stalks

Place the gammon in a very large saucepan. Fill with cold water, add the onion that has been roughly diced, the cinnamon, nutmeg, bay leaves, parsley stalks, peppercorns and 20 cloves. Bring to the boil, cover, and simmer for 2hrs 30 mins–3hrs depending on the size of your gammon.

When cooked, insert a metal skewer into the centre, and if the juices run clear then it is ready (I must at this point recommend buying a meat thermometer, a very useful tool in every kitchen). Carefully remove the gammon from the pan using two sturdy carving forks and place fat-side up in a roasting tray. With a sharp knife score the fat in a lattice pattern, evenly spread with honey, and insert a clove in the centre of each square in your lattice pattern. Place this in a preheated oven 180°C/350°F/gas 4 for 20–25 minutes until the glaze is golden brown.

Remove and cool for one hour then chill in a refrigerator for 24 hours before carving.

This is great with home made pickles and fresh baked bread.

Honey Glazed Chicken Stuffed with Apricots

This dish is so easy and can be prepared in advance for a dinner party, then roasted just twenty minutes before your guests arrive. We are very lucky to have our own bees here at Heligan and we use the honey in many different ways, including our Heligan Honey Ale, which is made by a small local brewery, served on draught in our own bar, or available in bottles to take away.

For 4

4 chicken breasts (skinless and boneless)
10 dried apricots
1 teaspoon of mixed spice
2 tablespoons of clear honey
1 teaspoon of English mustard
1 tablespoon of olive oil
8 sprigs of rosemary
pinch of salt

Split the chicken breasts lengthways and open out flat. Chop the dried apricots and place in the centre of each piece of chicken. Sprinkle with a little mixed spice and fold the top half over to encase the apricots. Mix together the honey, a pinch of salt, mustard, olive oil and half the rosemary (with the stalks removed) and stir until thoroughly blended.

Place the chicken on a greased roasting tin and spoon the honey mixture over the top. Roast in a moderately hot oven preheated to 200°C/400°F/gas 6 for 20–25 minutes until slightly caramelised on top, and garnish each with a sprig of rosemary.

This may be served as it is with a salad or if you intend to serve with potatoes and vegetables you may need a sauce with it. Here's a quick one you might try: make a gravy as you normally would and use it to de-glaze the pan you roasted the chicken in, then add a dash of port and a tablespoon of redcurrant jelly. Sounds simple, and it is.

Truffle Roasted Chicken

Unfortunately we do not have truffles growing here at Heligan and I had to buy them like everybody else. But as I did so it got me thinking 'I bet there are truffles around only we don't go looking for them in this country' – can you remember the last time you saw a pig being walked through the woods near you? Being a keen picker of wild mushrooms I can't help thinking these things. This recipe uses individual portions of chicken breast, but you could also use boneless thighs or even a whole chicken. Whatever you choose, the aroma of truffles makes this a most distinctive dish. Truffles are expensive but with cross-Channel travel being so cheap it gives us the ideal opportunity to bring back an ounce or two of black truffles, or white if you are feeling very extravagant.

For 4

4 boneless chicken breasts (with the skin still on)
30g/1oz black truffles
55g/2fl oz white truffle flavoured oil
290mls/10fl oz good chicken stock
110g/4oz chestnuts mushrooms, finely sliced
1 heaped tablespoon cornflour
3 tablespoons Madeira
1 tablespoon olive oil
salt and pepper
a little water

Rub the truffles clean with a soft cloth and slice as finely as you can. Try to get 20 thin slices at least. Lift the chicken skin away from the breast but leaving it still attached along one side. Make 5 cuts into the flesh, insert into each cut a slice of truffle, brush the flesh with truffle oil before replacing the skin back over the top. Place this on a baking tray that has been lightly brushed with truffle oil, brush the entire piece of chicken with more truffle oil before sprinkling with a little salt and pepper. Repeat for all of the chicken pieces, cling film over and refrigerate for 24 hours (this is not absolutely necessary but if you've paid good money for truffles then you want to get as much flavour and aroma out of them as possible and marinating in this way will certainly help). Roast in a preheated oven 220°C/425°F/gas 7 for 20–30 minutes until the skin is golden brown.

Serve with a mushroom and Madeira sauce, this is very simple – just fry the mushrooms in hot olive oil for 6 minutes, add the Madeira and stock, bring to the boil and thicken with cornflour mixed with a little water, stirring continuously as you add this to your sauce. Season to taste with a little salt and pepper.

Serve the chicken with the sauce underneath, as you do not want to mask the heady truffle aroma.

Grilled Chicken Rolled in Pesto

Basil is one of my favourite herbs and is the star of this dish. Without it this recipe just would not work. We are lucky to have an abundance of fresh basil close to hand and pesto is a good way of preserving that zing of fresh basil for use in winter months. This makes a wonderful lunch for people who don't want to compromise on depth of flavour while eating healthily.

For 4

4 skinless, boneless chicken breasts
a very large bunch of basil (at least 225g/8oz)
110g/4oz fresh Parmesan cheese
110/4oz pine nuts
150mls/5fl oz of olive oil
4 cloves of garlic
pinch of salt
1 small radicchio
1 bunch of watercress
1 bunch of rocket
1 lollo rosso

First make the pesto. Wash the basil, roughly chop and put in a food processor with the Parmesan (grated), pine-nuts, olive oil and a large pinch of salt. Whizz until it is a smooth paste. This is more than enough to coat the chicken, but I always make too much on purpose because it is so nice with pasta and it keeps well in an airtight jar in the fridge.

Brush the chicken with a little olive oil and grill for 8–12 minutes on each side. While this is going on, rip the salad leaves into a colander, rinse, shake dry and arrange on 4 plates. When the chicken is cooked, cut into thin strips, toss in a bowl and cover with enough pesto to evenly coat the chicken and neatly place on top of the leaves.

You do not need anything with this deliciously light lunch, but a nice cool glass of white wine complements it beautifully.

Chicken with White Wine and Capers

Capers are only very small things but they lift so many dishes. Wonderful with all kinds of fish, poultry and game, but not a very common ingredient. In fact some staff here at Heligan have never seen a caper before let alone tasted one – Tina, our bakery manager (having been vegetarian for 17 years) was most surprised with the sharp piquancy of capers and even more surprised when I casually mentioned 'You wouldn't think they were once crawling around would you?' (When it comes to veggies I just can't help myself being a tease). They are in fact the unopened flower buds from a Mediterranean shrub, which are then pickled. If you haven't tried them yet you really should – they are delicious!

For 4

8 boneless chicken thighs
2 tablespoons of olive oil
1 teaspoon paprika
1 onion, diced
55g/2oz button mushrooms, sliced
55g/2oz butter
55g/2oz plain flour
290mls/10fl oz good chicken stock
150mls/5fl oz double cream
150mls/5fl oz dry white wine
40 capers
1 tablespoon chopped fresh parsley
salt and pepper

Arrange the chicken thighs in a roasting tray, mix together the olive oil and paprika, then brush evenly over the chicken. Roast in a preheated oven 200°C/400°F/gas 6 for 30–35 minutes. In the meantime melt the butter in a saucepan, add the diced onion and fry gently for 5 minutes – add to this the flour and cook out for 3 minutes stirring continuously. Gradually add the stock drop by drop, stirring throughout to avoid lumps. When a smooth consistency is reached add the white wine, mushrooms and capers. Bring back to the boil and simmer gently for 10 minutes stirring continuously. Then add the cream and the parsley along with a little salt and pepper to taste. Your sauce is now finished.

Serve two thighs per portion with the white wine and caper sauce over the top – this would be great with a pilaff or sauté potatoes and fresh vegetables.

Poulet Picasso

A colourful chicken dish with Mediterranean influences, including a plethora of pungent fresh herbs, and both green and black olives. Most of the ingredients are to be found at Heligan, the onions, garlic, tomatoes and herbs. Unfortunately olives aren't grown here at Heligan; to find these one must travel a few miles east to the Eden Project, only I strongly suspect my scrumping would be frowned upon there. Shame though!

For 4

4 skinless, boneless chicken breasts
olive oil
8 tomatoes
85g/3oz finely chopped onion
2 teaspoons of tomato purée
5 cloves of garlic
12 pitted black olives
12 pitted green olives
splash of white wine
sprigs of: parsley, marjoram, basil, oregano, summer savory
salt and pepper

Heat the olive oil in a large sauté pan and fry the chicken breasts for 8 minutes on each side. Place the chicken on a hot plate, cover with foil and keep in a low oven while you make the sauce. Using the same pan used to fry the chicken, fry the chopped onions and crushed garlic until soft. Roughly chop the tomatoes, adding them to the pan along with the tomato purée and all the olives. Cook for 5 minutes adding just a splash of white wine. Then chop all the herbs quite finely and add to the sauce, keeping some back for garnish. Simmer and stir for a few minutes, taste and season if required.

Finally remove the chicken from the oven and slice each breast into 6 thin slices, fanning out each one on a warm plate, spoon over the tomato and olive sauce, sprinkle the remaining herbs on top and serve with a Caesar salad and crusty French bread, or perhaps a wild mushroom pilaff.

Chicken and Hog's Pudding Hot Pot

First of all hog's pudding is nothing to be afraid of. It is a Cornish delicately spiced sausage, traditionally served at breakfast time. Even if you are not a fan of black pudding, I urge you to give this a try – it is delicious. Mind you, I am a great fan of black pudding myself and cannot for the life of me understand anybody taking a dislike to it. It is food from the gods! I have seen a recipe for Lancashire hot pot which uses black pudding and this prompted me to make this dish using the local Cornish hog's pudding.

For 4

675g/1lb 8oz diced chicken
1 onion
2 cloves garlic
110g/4oz sliced mushrooms
570mls/1 pint chicken stock
1 tablespoon chopped fresh chives
2 tablespoons double cream
110g/4oz butter
55g/2oz plain flour
450g/1lb potatoes
110g/4oz hog's pudding
1 tablespoon olive oil
salt and pepper

Melt half the butter in a saucepan, finely chop the onion and garlic and gently fry for 5 minutes without colour. Add the mushrooms, chives and chicken and cook gently for a further 5 minutes.

In a separate pan melt the remaining butter, add the flour and cook for 3 minutes stirring continuously. To this slowly add the stock, drop by drop, stirring throughout until a smooth sauce has been made. Simmer this for 5 minutes then stir in the cream and season with salt and pepper to taste. Spread the chicken mixture evenly in a roasting pan or pie dish, pour the sauce over the top and set aside.

Wash and thinly slice the unpeeled potatoes, and then slice the hog's pudding to the same thickness. Arrange these on top of your hot pot, mixing the hog's pudding slices in with the sliced potatoes. Brush the potato with olive oil and bake in a preheated oven 200°C/400°F/gas 6 for 25–30 minutes until the potato is cooked and golden brown. Best served with braised red cabbage and buttery boiled potatoes and a glass of crisp dry white wine.

Traditional Rabbit Pie

Undoubtedly wild rabbit is far superior to farmed rabbit for flavour. Unfortunately as the age of a wild rabbit is an unknown factor and cooking times may vary, this must be remembered when following any recipe for rabbit. Most recipes for rabbit I have come across have the meat still on the bone. Now I don't know if it's me just being a bit of an old fuss pot, but finding bones in a pie just doesn't seem right. So my recipe is without bones but if you are a stickler for tradition, by all means leave them in – just don't forget to tell your guests!

For 4–6

1 x 1.35kg/3lb rabbit (approx)
1 large onion
4 rashers of smoked streaky bacon
1 pint of game or chicken stock
290mls/10fl oz medium dry cider
110g/4oz carrot
110g/4oz dry pitted prunes
6 bay leaves
1 teaspoon chopped fresh sage
55g/2oz butter
55g/2oz plain flour (plus a little more for dusting)
285g/10oz ready to roll puff pastry
1 beaten egg
salt and pepper

Chop your rabbit into 5 large chunks, place in a large saucepan, followed by the stock, cider, bay, sage and a little salt and pepper. Bring to the boil and simmer. Add to this the peeled and diced onion, the peeled and sliced carrot, cover with a lid and simmer for at least 2 hours or until meat is falling from the bone. During this time top up with water if the liquid has evaporated too much. When the rabbit is cooked, remove from the pan and allow to cool. Also remove all pieces of carrot and onion with a slotted spoon. Pass the remaining liquor through a fine sieve into a jug. In a clean saucepan melt the butter, add the flour and cook out for 3 minutes stirring continuously. Then gradually add the liquor, drop by drop, stirring throughout. When a smooth sauce is reached, taste and season with salt and pepper.

With the rabbit now cool remove all the meat from the bones, arrange this in a pie dish with the onion and carrot that you have saved and the roughly chopped prunes. Then pour on the sauce, stopping just below the rim of the pie dish and keeping any remaining sauce to serve with the finished pie. Roll out the puff pastry just a little larger than the pie dish and carefully drape over the top. Trim off any excess pastry from the sides and crimp around the edge with your finger and thumb. Brush the top with beaten egg, pierce the centre with a knife and bake in a preheated oven 190°C/375°F/gas 5 for 25–30 minutes until puffed and golden brown. Serve with a generous amount of buttery mashed potato and some minted fresh garden peas.

Duck Breasts with Greengage and Sage

A surfeit of greengages and an abundance of fresh sage led to the invention of this dish. Our local butcher provided us with the plumpest duck breasts. Pan-fried and juicy with a compote of greengage and sage and accompanied by a 'game jus' – it makes me hungry just describing it here!

For 4

4 plump, boneless duck breasts (with skin)
55g/2oz plain flour
285g/10oz greengages
55g/2oz caster sugar
55g/2oz fresh sage
2 tablespoons sunflower oil
425mls/15fl oz of game stock (or chicken stock)
heaped tablespoon cornflour
a little water
salt and pepper

Firstly wash and remove the stones from the greengages, heat in a pan with just a splash of water and the sugar. When the fruit is soft, pass through a sieve to remove the skins, leaving a smooth fruit pulp. Finely chop the sage and add half to the fruit. Mix the other half into the stock and bring to the boil. Thicken with cornflour mixed with a little water, season to taste and simmer gently.

Heat the oil in a large frying pan, roll the duck breasts in plain flour with a pinch of salt, and when the oil is smoking fry the duck breasts skin-side down for 5 minutes, then turn and cook the other side also for 5 minutes. By this time the duck breasts should be golden brown but pink in the middle. Remove from the heat and rest for 2 minutes. Slice each breast into 6 slices, fan out on a hot plate, accompanied by a spoonful of fruit compôte and a cordon of 'game jus' around the meat. Serve with buttery new potatoes and crisp lightly cooked vegetables.

Mangetout, Julienne carrots and baby King Edwards went very well when we cooked this succulent dish for one of our Feast Nights.

The Perfect Brace of Roast Pheasants

On no account do I advocate the running down of unsuspecting pheasants or the ridiculing of innocent vegetarians but... a funny thing happened to me on the way to work one morning, while giving a vegetarian colleague a lift. A pheasant darted out of the undergrowth and hit my bumper with quite a thud. My passenger yelled out in a hysterical panic as the injured bird flapped about in the road – so, taking control of the situation, I caught the bird, swiftly wrung its neck and popped it into the boot of the car. I was already planning what sort of sauce to serve with it when I realised my passenger was in a serious state of shock and spent the rest of the day drinking sweet tea for his nerves. The pheasant was delicious, nevertheless!

For 4–6

2 medium oven ready pheasants
(ideally 1 male, 1 female)
2 medium cooking apples
110g/4oz butter
8 slices smoked streaky bacon
salt and pepper

For Gravy:
30g/1oz plain flour
1 tablespoon redcurrant jelly
2 tablespoons red wine or port
salt and pepper

Take your pheasants, rinse under a cold tap and remove any remaining feathers. Place in a large roasting pan with 1cm/half inch water. Spread the butter over the pheasants' breasts and thighs before placing 4 rashers of bacon to cover the breasts (when shopping for the bacon think 'the fattier the better'). Cut the apples into large wedges and insert into your bird by the Parson's Nose end. All this will help your bird stay moist and prevent it drying out during cooking. Sprinkle with a large pinch of salt and pepper, then roast in a preheated oven 200°C/400°F/gas 6 for 60–70 minutes, depending on the weight of your birds. Baste frequently. To be on the safe side make a cut just behind the thigh all the way to the bone – if there is any trace of blood, cook for a little longer.

When cooked, lift the pheasants from the pan and set aside for a few minutes. Place the pan over a medium heat, add a little water and skim any excess fat with a ladle. Sprinkle flour onto the roasting juices stirring continuously. Now add the redcurrant jelly and red wine, stirring until the jelly has dissolved, season to taste and pass through a fine sieve into a sauce boat.

Carve the pheasants and serve the sauce separately, – perfect with roast potatoes and a glass of red wine.

Guinea Fowl with Sun Dried Tomato and Basil

Most of our guinea fowl these days are not wild game birds but a semi-domestic breed. This has in turn lowered the price, made the meat more accessible, and because the age of the birds is known, this makes sure the meat is tender. I have found guinea fowl to be more reliable than pigeon or pheasant – always being plump, moist with no hint of toughness. The taste is that of a slightly more gamey chicken – the flesh being only a shade darker than chicken. In fact, one of our gardeners at Heligan exclaimed earnestly 'That was the best chicken I've ever tasted'.

For 4

4 x 140g–170g/5–6oz guinea fowl breasts
(boneless and skinless)
4 rashers of rindless back bacon
12 sun dried tomatoes in oil
20 large basil leaves
2 tablespoons olive oil
570mls/1pint game or chicken stock
1 heaped tablespoon cornflour
a little water

Cut with a sharp knife along one side of each breast, quite deeply to form a pocket. Into each pocket insert 2 sun dried tomatoes, then wrap each breast neatly with a rasher of bacon around the middle with the loose end tucked underneath. Take a baking sheet and brush with a little oil, then arrange the guinea fowl breasts on it and brush liberally with olive oil. Roast in a pre-heated oven 200°C/400°F/gas 6 for 25–30 minutes.

Then heat the game stock in a saucepan, wipe the remaining sun dried tomatoes with kitchen towel to remove excess oil, dice finely and add to the stock. Shred the basil, adding most of this to the stock but keeping some back for garnish later. When the stock is simmering mix the cornflour with some water, then slowly add to the stock, stirring continuously to avoid lumps. Stop when you are happy with the consistency (it should be a gravy of medium thickness). Simmer gently for a further 2 minutes, then use straightaway to avoid cooking the basil for too long.

Place each breast on a chopping board and slice into 5 or 6 pieces, fan these out on one half of each of 4 dinner plates and ladle some sauce over the top, followed by a sprinkle of shredded basil. Serve with Dauphinoise potatoes (see A *Taste of Heligan – vegetarian and fruit recipes*) and some fresh garden peas and baby carrots.

Poacher's Purse

Poacher's purse is a dish with endless variations, using any mixture of game, depending on the season. The meat can be varied just as long as you adjust the cooking time accordingly. If your meat has been shot, be careful to remove all the pellets; although having said that, in my experience many diners seem quite pleased when they find a piece of shot – it lends authenticity to the dish!

For 4

675g/1lb 8oz mixed boneless diced game
(e.g. venison, rabbit, pheasant)
1 tablespoon sunflower oil
1 large diced onion
170g/6oz sliced Portobello mushrooms
1 clove of garlic
1 tablespoon chopped fresh parsley
290mls/10fl oz real ale
290mls/10fl oz good game stock
(or a good chicken stock)
2 tablespoons tomato purée
1 heaped tablespoon cornflour
a little water
salt and pepper
340g/12oz ready to roll puff pastry
1 beaten egg
plain flour for dusting
4 sprigs rosemary

Heat the oil in a large saucepan, add the diced game and fry for 10 minutes, stirring to ensure even browning. Add the onion, garlic and sliced mushrooms and cook for a further 5 minutes. Then pour the stock and the beer over the game and add the parsley, tomato purée and a little salt and pepper. Bring to the boil and simmer until the meat is tender. This may take you between 1–3hrs depending on the age and type of game you use. When the meat is tender, skim away any fat from the top with a ladle. Then thicken with cornflour mixed with a splash of water, stirring continuously as you add this to your saucepan; only use as much as you need to reach the desired thickness. Season to taste and leave on a very low heat to keep hot.

Roll out the puff pastry on a floured table and cut into 4 x 12cm/5inch semi-circles, brush with beaten egg, place on a lightly greased baking sheet and bake in a preheated oven 200°C/400°F/gas 6 for 20–25 minutes or until puffed and golden brown. Cut each through the middle, placing the bottom halves onto four warm plates. Ladle a good measure of meat on the top of each, then place the other half of the puff pastry on the top. Garnish with a sprig of rosemary and serve with roast potatoes, some young crisp vegetables and a glass of real ale.

Venison with Shallots and Red Wine

Recently I have adapted this recipe to cook rabbit, pheasant, guinea fowl and even a Black Silky – this is one of the breeds of fowl we have here at Heligan – a very fluffy jet-black chicken that is often admired. I was given one of these handsome fellows ready for the oven – so, eager to try something new, I took it home with me and that night for supper a Black Silky along with some home-grown shallots and a splash of claret was cooked slowly in the Rayburn. It smelt divine and tasted slightly gamier than normal chicken. Unfortunately though, as it turned out, not only were the feathers black, but the skin and bones were black and the flesh was a little on the grey side too!

For 4

675g/1lb 8oz lean diced venison
340g/12 oz small, peeled shallots
2 cloves of garlic
150mls/5fl oz of red wine
290mls/10fl oz of chicken stock
1 tablespoon tomato purée
225g/8oz tomatoes
small sprigs of: parsley, rosemary, sage
4 bay leaves
2 teaspoons paprika
1 tablespoon of sunflower oil
salt and pepper
1 tablespoon of cornflour (if required)
splash of water

Take a large pan with a tight-fitting lid – for use on the top and inside the oven – and heat the oil until just smoking, then seal the meat evenly on all sides. Turn down the heat and add the whole shallots, crushed garlic, paprika, all the herbs, finely chopped and a little salt and pepper. Cook this for 5 minutes.

Next pour in the red wine, add the chicken stock, a tablespoon of tomato purée and the roughly chopped tomatoes. Bring to the boil and simmer – other ingredients may be added at this point, for example chopped peppers, button mushrooms or diced root vegetables.

Cover with the lid and place in the oven at quite a low temperature – 170°C/325°F/gas 3. The cooking time may vary between one and a half and three hours, depending on the cut and tenderness of your venison. The only way to tell is to taste periodically during the cooking process. Also keep an eye on liquid level and top up with a splash of boiling water if required.

When cooked, if you find the sauce needs to be thickened, do this with the cornflour mixed with a little water and stir in slowly, using only as much as you need. Finally, taste and adjust the seasoning if required and serve.

Serve with roast potatoes and lightly cooked seasonal vegetables, or a pilaff would go very well.

Postscript

It is now fourteen years since the restoration of the Lost Gardens of Heligan began.

At first it was a great adventure into the past, driven by archaeological rather than horticultural curiosity. Within days of entering the Lost Gardens for the first time, Tim Smit and John Nelson hacked their way into what was the Melon Yard, the heart of the productive gardens and discovered the signatures left by the garden staff of August 1914, most of whom had subsequently departed for the battlefields in France. The early restoration was driven, first, by their desire to restore the structures of the working buildings and glasshouses as a memorial to these men and then by the realisation that we should, still more importantly, be celebrating their purpose.

Since then, the demonstration of best practice by our own staff in the Vegetable, Melon and Flower Gardens and the production of traditional crops for harvest around the year, to be consumed, fresh, in season, on site, have tapped a rich vein of interest from our visitors. With the ever-growing concern about contemporary food production and safety, our helping to remind the public of a different way – the pleasures attached to eating flavoursome, local food with full traceability – has proved a thoroughly worthwhile activity.

The most recent aspect of the project here has been to move out into the Heligan estate and run our own flock, herd and pigs, which are now served from the restaurant on an occasional basis. To all Paul's thanks to those for making this all possible, I would like to add my own – to Terry, Richard and Ian Lobb, who have helped us along a steep learning curve.

Candy Smit